ANIMAL IDIOMS

Birdbrain: Are Birds Dumb?

BY LAURA PERDEW

CONTENT CONSULTANT
PETER PATON, PhD
PROFESSOR AND CHAIR,
DEPARTMENT OF NATURAL
RESOURCES SCIENCE
UNIVERSITY OF RHODE ISLAND

Kids Core
An Imprint of Abdo Publishing
abdobooks.com

abdobooks.com

Published by Abdo Publishing, a division of ABDO, PO Box 398166, Minneapolis, Minnesota 55439. Copyright © 2022 by Abdo Consulting Group, Inc. International copyrights reserved in all countries. No part of this book may be reproduced in any form without written permission from the publisher. Kids Core™ is a trademark and logo of Abdo Publishing.

Printed in the United States of America, North Mankato, Minnesota.
102021
012022

THIS BOOK CONTAINS RECYCLED MATERIALS

Cover Photos: Tracy Starr/Shutterstock Images, (bird); Shutterstock Images, (background)
Interior Photos: Shutterstock Images, 4–5, 26; Vincent St. Thomas/iStockphoto, 6; Aldona Griskeviciene/Shutterstock Images, 8; iStockphoto, 10–11, 16–17; Rob Palmer Photography/Shutterstock Images, 12; Jiri Hrebicek/Shutterstock Images, 14; Malisa Nicolau/Shutterstock Images, 19; Jean-Paul Ferrero/Auscape International/Alamy, 21; Karel Gallas/Shutterstock Images, 22–23; Oakland Images/Shutterstock Images, 25; JMx Images/Shutterstock Images, 28 (top); Ben Schonewille/Shutterstock Images, 28 (bottom); Thierry Van Baelinghem/Science Source, 29 (top); Frank Fichtmueller/Shutterstock Images, 29 (bottom)

Editor: Christine Ha
Series Designer: Katharine Hale

Library of Congress Control Number: 2021941225

Publisher's Cataloging-in-Publication Data

Names: Perdew, Laura, author.
Title: Birdbrain: are birds dumb? / by Laura Perdew
Other title: are birds dumb?
Description: Minneapolis, Minnesota : Abdo Publishing, 2022 | Series: Animal idioms | Includes online resources and index.
Identifiers: ISBN 9781532196652 (lib. bdg.) | ISBN 9781644946442 (pbk.) | ISBN 9781098218461 (ebook)
Subjects: LCSH: Birds--Juvenile literature. | Birds--Behavior--Juvenile literature. | Animal intelligence--Juvenile literature. | Animal instinct--Juvenile literature. | Idiomatic expressions--Juvenile literature.
Classification: DDC 598.2--dc23

CONTENTS

CHAPTER 1
Bird Tricks 4

CHAPTER 2
Communication 10

CHAPTER 3
Problem Solving 16

CHAPTER 4
Good Memory 22

Bird Facts 28
Glossary 30
Online Resources 31
Learn More 31
Index 32
About the Author 32

Having a pet bird can be a lot of fun.

Bird Tricks

Risa couldn't wait to show her new parrot, Max, to her best friend. But when Diego saw Max, he asked, "Why not a dog? You can teach them tricks. That parrot is just a birdbrain!"

"You can teach birds tricks, too," Risa replied. "Watch this!"

Many birds, such as parrots, can be trained to do cool tricks.

Risa turned on some music. Max gave a chirp and started dancing! He swayed back and forth. He flapped his wings. He even bobbed his head and stomped his feet to the beat.

Diego was impressed. He didn't know birds could recognize music and even dance. Risa said, "See? Birds aren't dumb! Birds are smart!"

What Are Idioms?

Birdbrain is an example of an idiom. An idiom is an expression that is often used in a specific language. It usually means something other than the words that make up the idiom. *Birdbrain* describes someone who is not very smart. Diego called the parrot a birdbrain because he believed it wasn't smart.

Intelligence versus Instinct

Intelligence is having the ability to learn and to understand. Instinct is a natural behavior that is not learned. Birds are intelligent. They have shown the ability to learn and understand. They change their behavior based on past experiences.

Bird Brain versus Human Brain

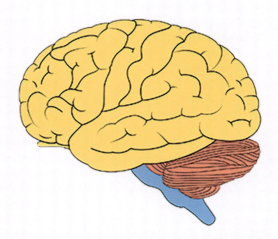

**Average parrot brain
8 ounces (250 g)**

**Average human brain
44 ounces (1,250 g)**

Birds have small brains compared to humans. But their brains are packed with neurons. This helps birds perform many tasks, including solving problems, using tools, and even imitating and communicating with humans.

But are birds really simple-minded? A bird's brain is small. But size may not be as important as what's inside the brain. **Neurons** are nerve cells that carry messages within the brain.

There are a lot of neurons packed in a bird's small brain.

Corvids and parrots are at the top of the class when it comes to bird intelligence. Scientists have discovered that these birds have an excellent memory. They also can solve problems and use tools.

Further Evidence

Look at the website below. Does it give any new evidence to support Chapter One?

Bird Brains

abdocorelibrary.com/birdbrain

Sometimes, birds communicate visually. For example, some birds show off their feathers, puff up, or dance to attract mates.

Communication

Birds tweet, hoot, sing, caw, crow, and make many other noises to communicate. Each sound means something different. They might be trying to find a mate. They could be warning others of a nearby **predator**. They might be defending their territory.

When a chickadee hears a warning call from another chickadee, it will freeze in place until it hears the "all clear" call.

Bird Song

Birds learn their songs much like children learn to speak. When baby birds are still in the nest, they listen to the adults around them. Once they leave the nest, they must practice getting their calls and songs right.

Some birds, such as chickadees, have very complicated calls. One is an alarm. This *chicka-dee-dee-dee* call tells others about a nearby predator. The more *dees* at the end of the call, the larger and more **threatening** the predator is. Even other species of birds listen to the warning.

Using Human Words

Birds have even learned to speak using human words. Parrots are especially good at this. Not only can they learn words, but they can also use them correctly.

Each flock of wild parrots creates its own unique songs. This allows birds of the same flock to recognize each other.

Birds can even answer questions. Some parrots have put together new phrases using words they already know.

Alex the Parrot

In the 1970s, Dr. Irene Pepperberg began working with an African grey parrot named Alex. She taught him more than 100 English words. Alex could name colors and shapes. Also, he could count to eight and do many other tasks.

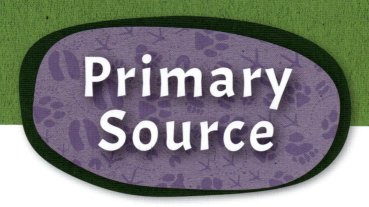

Primary Source

Dr. Irene Pepperberg taught the African grey parrot Alex many English words. In an interview about Alex and other parrots, she said:

> These birds are doing things that in some cases are equivalent to 5- and 6-year-old children. . . . So, why? How? What could that tell us about our brains?

Source: Rebecca Boyle. "How Irene Pepperberg Revolutionized Our Understanding of Bird Intelligence." *Audubon*, 27 Mar. 2018, audubon.org. Accessed 6 July 2021.

Comparing Texts

Think about the quote. Does this quote support the information in this chapter? Or does it give a different perspective? Explain how in two to three sentences.

Scientists believe corvids, such as crows, are some of the most intelligent animals in the world.

Problem Solving

Birds have proven to be good problem solvers in many studies. For example, scientists observed that some carrion crows in Japan place nuts on roads. They wait for cars to drive by and crush the shells. Once the nuts are cracked open, the birds eat them.

Sometimes, the crows even wait for the red light to stop traffic before flying to grab the nuts!

Solving Puzzles

One study tested a group of cockatoos' problem-solving skills. The researchers put a nut in a locked box. To get the treats, the cockatoos had to open five locks. Each lock was different, and they had to be opened in a certain order. One of the birds opened all the locks with no training. Most of the birds were able to solve the puzzle after watching a demonstration or trying it a few times. This study showed that birds can learn and remember. They understand cause and effect.

Scientists believe cockatoos are about as smart as human four-year-olds.

Making Tools

Using tools was once something scientists thought only humans and primates did.

But in a study, a New Caledonian crow named Betty bent a piece of wire in her cage into a hook. She used it to pluck a treat out of a plastic tube.

Scientists discovered that wild crows also use tools to get food. Researchers captured several wild crows. Then, the researchers observed that most of the birds made hooks out of sticks to get food out of logs. This showed that crows know how to use tools to solve problems.

007 at Work

Dr. Alex Taylor set up an eight-step puzzle for a New Caledonian crow named 007. Each step needed a tool to move on to the next step. 007 solved the puzzle and retrieved his treat in under three minutes.

Crows can make tools by bending sticks with their beaks.

Explore Online

Visit the website below. Does it give any new information about crows and how scientists have worked with them?

New Caledonian Crow Lab

abdocorelibrary.com/birdbrain

The seeds that birds do not return to may grow into trees. Birds are important in keeping forests strong.

CHAPTER 4

Good Memory

Every fall, birds collect and stash thousands of seeds in different places. For example, a nutcracker bird can collect as many as 33,000 pine seeds in a day and bury them in more than 2,500 different **caches**. But how do they remember where all their seeds are?

Birds have excellent memory. Many bird brains have a large hippocampus. This part of the brain helps with learning and memory.

Recognizing Faces

Some birds, such as crows, can remember faces. In one experiment, a scientist wore a mask when he captured and marked seven wild crows. The crows were then released. For years afterward,

Sense of Time

In an experiment, scrub jays were given wax worms. They hid the worms to eat later. For a couple days, the birds returned to eat the worms. But after five days, they stopped returning. The birds knew the worms had begun to decay. This showed that the birds understood the passage of time.

Crows are very social. They play with and learn from one another.

anyone wearing the mask was attacked by the crows in the area. People not wearing the mask were left alone. Unmarked crows also joined in attacking masked people. They learned to recognize danger from the other crows.

Some birds can remember and interact with the humans who refill bird feeders.

Birdbrain?

The idea that birds are not smart is incorrect. Birds are among Earth's smartest creatures and can communicate with each other and with humans. They can solve problems, plan, and use tools. Birds learn from watching others. The term *birdbrain* shouldn't be an insult. It should be a compliment!

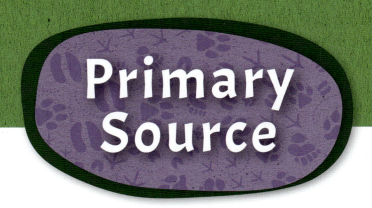

Writer Peter Friederici writes about nutcracker birds' use of food storage:

> But more remarkable than the . . . energy nutcrackers invest in storing food is their success at recovering it. . . . Nutcrackers and their young may still be eating stored seeds a year after burying them.

Source: Peter Friederici. "The Bird That Never Forgets." *National Wildlife Federation*, Oct. 2000, nwf.org. Accessed 6 July 2021.

What's the Big Idea?

Read the quote carefully. What is its main idea? Explain how the main idea is supported by details, naming two or three of those supporting details.

Bird Facts

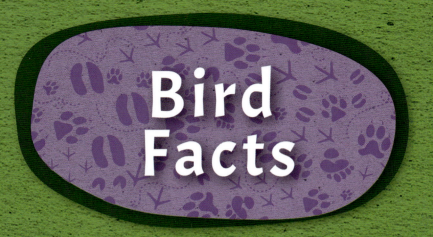

Birds communicate with each other by using different sounds for different situations.

Some birds have been taught to use human words.

Crows can make and use tools to solve problems.

Birds have excellent memory and can remember where they stashed seeds.

29

Glossary

caches
stores of extra food animals hide for future use

corvids
birds of the crow family, including ravens, crows, jays, magpies, rooks, and jackdaws

intelligence
the ability to understand, think, and learn

neurons
nerve cells that carry messages

predator
an animal that hunts other animals for food

threatening
something that is dangerous and might cause harm

Online Resources

To learn more about birds, visit our free resource websites below.

Visit **abdocorelibrary.com** or scan this QR code for free Common Core resources for teachers and students, including vetted activities, multimedia, and booklinks, for deeper subject comprehension.

Visit **abdobooklinks.com** or scan this QR code for free additional online weblinks for further learning. These links are routinely monitored and updated to provide the most current information available.

Learn More

Huddleston, Emma. *How Birds Fly*. Abdo, 2021.

Murray, Julie. *Parrots*. Abdo, 2020.

Zommer, Yuval. *The Big Book of Birds*. Thames & Hudson, 2019.

Index

caches, 23
chickadees, 13
cockatoos, 18
crows, 9, 17–18, 20, 21,
   24–25

Friederici, Peter, 27

idioms, 5, 7, 26

Japan, 17

neurons, 8–9
nutcracker birds, 23, 27

parrots, 5–6, 7, 8, 9, 13–14, 15
Pepperberg, Irene, 14, 15
predators, 11, 13

scrub jays, 24
studies, 17, 18, 20, 24–25

Taylor, Alex, 20

About the Author

Laura Perdew is a mom, writing consultant, and author of
more than 40 books for children. She writes both fiction
and nonfiction with a focus on nature, the environment,
and environmental issues. She lives and plays in
Boulder, Colorado.